W9-AHF-459

SHIFTING GEARS

A BRAIN-BASED APPROACH
TO ENGAGING YOUR BEST SELF

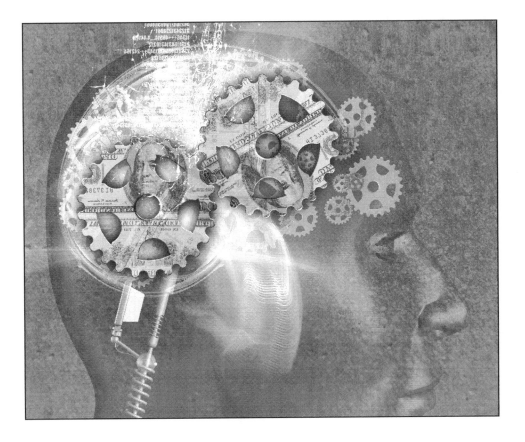

ROBIN ROSE

Shifting Gears
A Brain-Based Approach to Engaging Your Best Self

Copyright © 2010 Robin Rose

All rights reserved.

ISBN 978-0-9669108-2-7

A heartfelt thank you to my friends and family. They have supported my passion for learning, understanding and growth, and have contributed immeasurably to my work. In particular, thank you to Lisa Latin – friend, editor, and producer. Without her drive, this book might still be just an idea!

StayWell Press
a division of

ROBIN ROSE
TRAINING & CONSULTING

3760 Market St. NE, #132
Salem, Oregon 97301

(503) 873-3649

For more info and to sign-up for the free
StayWell newsletter, please visit:

www.RobinRose.com

Contents

Putting It All Together............................115
[make life easier]
Including:

Introduction

Introduction
[start here]

Do you find yourself getting really irritated with other people, or impatient when you're driving? Do you tend to get frustrated at work? Do you have a habit of worrying about things? Do you feel exhausted way too often? Or overwhelmed? What about headaches, heart-burn, or low-back pain – are they a regular part of your life? Do you see yourself as being a "negative" person? Do other people see you that way?

If you answered "Yes" to any of these questions, this book is for you!

With a surprisingly small investment of time and effort (just a little more than it takes to read this book), you will learn to make some very useful connections. You'll discover how your breathing and your tendency to worry affect how you sleep at night, how you move through your day, and what moods you get into — at work and at home. You'll discover how your physical health is impacted. Most importantly, you will learn how easily you can make simple shifts that will dissolve that neck tension, erase those negative moods, and dispel your worry.

This book will help you understand how your brain works and what is required for you to maintain focus, balance, and health. It all boils down to one concept and four skills.

One Concept: Understand how your brain works

Four Skills:

1. Breathe (effectively)

2. Choose your self-talk

3. Repair your injured relationships

4. Feel your feelings (but act from your values)

This book is full of information that will help you develop greater understanding and some very useful skills. As you apply what you're learning, you'll find yourself living with greater balance, sanity, and ease. You'll like yourself and other people more. You'll feel better at the end of the day.

I've been teaching people how to make positive changes in their lives for 25 years. The skills and strategies presented here are the core concepts that really work. People regularly contact me with stories of monumental positive changes that resulted from engaging this learning. I trust that you, too, will find what you need in here.

My intention is that this information brings you deeper levels of satisfaction and calm, and that you find openings to greater health, fun, and joy. Your life is made up of millions of moments. As you shift the moment you are having right now, the next moment is also changed, and the next, and eventually the overall pattern of your life. This book provides tools you can use to make those shifts in *any* moment.

Brain Basics

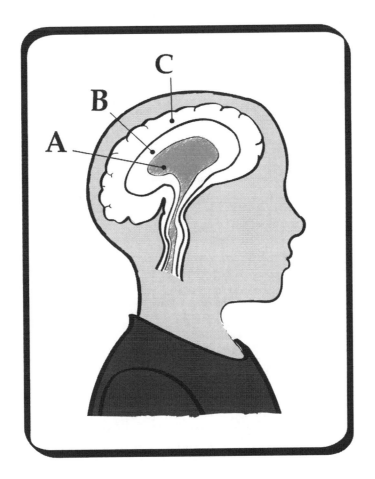

Brain Basics
[know what you're working with]

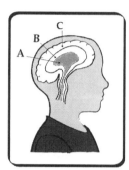

One of the truly wonderful things about being human is that we come complete with brains that are perfectly geared to do whatever we need them to do. Sometimes our brains are focused on details and numbers, and at other times they're focused on learning a new skill or generating some form of creative expression. Our brains are amazingly versatile. You could think of your brain as a perfect engine – one that shifts gears quickly and easily, as needed… it's all about meeting the different needs inherent in different situations.

Among the many needs that our brains address every day, there is one that stands above all the rest. *We all inherently embody the most primary need: the need to survive.* It is absolutely, hands down, the most important drive we humans have. Your brain knows this. Your brain knows that its prime directive is to keep you alive.

Conveniently, your brain is perfectly built to fulfill this mission. You have a "survival brain" that is exquisitely geared for the job. Most of the time you don't have any awareness of its existence, but you can rest assured that it is indeed there, on call 24/7 – ready for action.

Your survival brain is always ready to jump into action and fend off any potential threat to your survival – real or imagined.

Most people get at least some practice shifting into and out of their survival brain every single day. It happens all the time, for each and every one of us. What does this shift into the survival brain look like? Have you ever found yourself in some version of this scenario?

You leave work feeling satisfied with your day. Your schedule was full, but with a little extra effort you got everything done, and you're out the door in time to get to your daughter's soccer game – on time, for the first time in weeks. Yeah!

Traffic looks manageable, and you settle in for the commute. But within minutes traffic is getting bad, and you're crawling along in the thick of it. Time check. Relief. It's tight, but you're still okay.

*Then, all of a sudden, some guy cuts right in front of you – and he nearly clipped you!! And of course he's not using any turn signals. You blast him at the top of your lungs, "You *!#&* idiot!! Where'd you learn to drive?!" Grrr... You managed to avoid having an accident, but now you're rattled. And peeved. Then* *he starts driving way too slow, and you can't get over. Your blood is starting to boil. What a jerk!*

You give him a few of your favorite gestures, but you can't get any satisfaction because he's oblivious. He's yakking away on a cell phone. Geez, you would think people could get a clue.

The traffic is getting really bad, and you're feeling that headache you've kept at bay all day is coming back. You're kicking yourself for not leaving earlier. You know there would have been a lot less traffic. And now you can feel your neck is getting so tight you can barely turn your head.

As you're creeping along, the disappointment starts settling in. And then the guilt. Oh, look how late it's getting. There is no way you are going to make it. You're gonna be late. Again.

And then you start anticipating the lecture later on tonight, going on about how you work too much and family priorities. Oh, why can't anyone see that you really are trying? Are you ever gonna get a break?!

Does this incident sound in any way familiar? In just a few brief moments everything can turn from being pretty okay to such a big mess. Then you're left feeling frustrated... or angry... plus you've also got a headache, or maybe an upset stomach, or your neck is getting stiff.

Let's look at what happened to generate this shift from well-being to distress so quickly.

Remember, your brain's main job is survival. It's always looking out for you, and it's more concerned with keeping you alive than figuring out the answer to whatever is the seemingly important question of the moment.

When you have worried or fear-based thoughts and become emotionally worked up, your brain reads this as a threat – and that perception of threat activates your survival brain.

As soon as the survival mechanism takes over, any of the systems in your body not needed for immediate survival will shut down. By shutting down, all of your attention can be directed to overcoming the perceived threat.

Whether that threat is being late to the soccer game or being mowed down in traffic or being yelled at by your boss, the outcome is pretty much the same: anger, frustration, anxiety, body tension, and pain – physical or emotional.

This book will help you understand more about when and how *your* particular brain shifts gears. As your understanding grows, so will your ability to stop, assess, and manage your thinking, moods, and behaviors.

Let's start by imagining the brain. We'll use a simple model that divides the brain into three sections:

Thinking Brain (Responding)

- *Also known as cerebral cortex or learning brain*
- *Newest addition – last area to fully develop, typically by age 24-26*
- *Can stay calm in the midst of upset*
- *Can predict consequences of own actions*
- *Used for problem solving, critical thinking, reflection, and creativity*
- *Impulse control and self-reflection abilities*
- *Presumes and focuses on creating success*

Emotional Brain (Relating)

- *Also known as the limbic system, located in the middle of your brain*
- *Involved with emotions, memory, and motivation*
- *Responsible for autonomic functions and homeostasis*
- *Automatically connects and relates to other people's limbic systems, resulting in emotional contagion*

Survival Brain (Reacting)

- *Also known as reptilian or primitive brain*
- *Oldest part – located at the base of your brain*
- *Used for survival functions, respiration, and elimination*
- *Activated by fear and/or pain*
- *No thinking, self-awareness, or impulse control*
- *96% developed by age three*

Thinking

Emotional

Survival

Each section of the brain has its particular strengths, abilities, functions, and limitations. The *thinking* brain creates, reflects, projects, and problem solves. The *emotional* brain maintains internal stability, emotionally and physically. It also regulates motivation and various homeostatic functions, including body temperature and appetite. The *survival* brain manages basic bodily functions such as respiration, digestion, circulation, and elimination. It also provides you with superhuman strength in crisis moments, in case you need to lift a car or sprint for help when usually you can't jog half a block.

Where we foul up is in trying to use the wrong tool for the job. For example:

- Engaging the survival brain when thinking brain skills would work better. *All impulsive reactions fall in this category.*

- Engaging the thinking brain when emotional brain skills are needed. *For example, using logic when an emotional connection is called for.*

- Engaging the thinking brain when a survival brain reaction is needed. *For example, suppose your toddler is on his tricycle – headed for the busy street. Yikes! It's necessary to react immediately to avert an accident. No need to stop and choose what shoes to put on… Forget the shoes... Go! Now!*

We need to use the part of the brain that fits the task at hand. Yet – all too often – we engage our survival brain when what we really need are thinking brain skills and solutions.

How can you tell which part of your brain you're using? It's simple – just watch how you respond when you're trying to relate and things don't go your way:

Survival Brain	Thinking Brain
Critical / Disrespectful	Curious / Compassionate
"I'm Right!!!"	Listens / Considers other perspectives
Rigid / Controlling	Creative / Adaptive
Overwhelmed	Optimistic / Resilient
Focused on blaming	Focused on solutions
Argumentative / Dramatic	Collaborative / Supportive
Personalizes	Does not personalize
Chronic pain / Fatigue	Healthy / Energetic
Irritable / Humorless	Can find the humor
Recycles the story or issue	Lets go / Moves forward
Reactive / Complaining	Proactive / Requesting

Here are some examples of common behaviors associated with survival brain reactions:

- *Saying mean or hurtful things to people we love*

- *Being critical – shaming and blaming*

- *Oblivious to or not concerned with others' needs*

- *Withholding information*

- *Being secretive or dishonest*

- *Recycling events without resolving them*

- *Accusing, complaining*

- *Sulking, shutting down*

- *Competing, comparing*

- *Gossiping, snide remarks*

- *Mean-spirited jokes*

- *Impatience*

- *Stomping off*

Evidence suggests that people react from their survival brains 70 - 90% of the time!

The Downward Spiral

Here's the bottom line: when you downshift into your survival brain, you cannot think, relate, listen, or communicate effectively.

You may want to, but you simply cannot do it. Nobody can. The survival brain is not set up to handle those sorts of functions.

Consequently, when we are operating from our survival brain, we regularly damage personal and professional relationships, in addition to our own health. In survival mode we're not able to access our rational skill set, so we're not as effective, focused, or accurate. We lose access to our best skills.

Why is it that we end up in our survival brain so often?

The answer is surprisingly simple. When you feel irritated or stressed, or if you get surprised (happily or not), you're very likely to hold your breath. It's a normal human startle response.

But here's the catch: when you hold your breath, that automatically sends a message to your brain that something is wrong, so your brain immediately gets busy doing what it's designed to do: help you survive. (*Remember, your brain's number one job is to keep you safe.*)

Within eight seconds of holding your breath, your brain releases the chemicals it thinks you'll need in order to survive the perceived threat. Once those chemicals are released, your brain has downshifted into survival mode – and it all occurs within eight seconds.

This downward spiral is a simple yet powerful sequence – one we all go through (most often unconsciously) many times every day.

Now here's the good news:

As you start to practice using the skills and strategies suggested in this book, you'll expand your self-awareness and you'll develop the ability to recognize, interrupt, and reroute your downward spirals. Over time, you'll begin to notice that actually eight seconds *is* enough time. In eight seconds...

▶ you *can* remember to breathe

▶ you *can* stop the downward spiral

▶ you *can* stay in your thinking brain

8 *seconds is enough time to change your mind*

Look and Listen

One way to develop more self-awareness is to notice your tone of voice and body… you'll find clues as to what gear you're in:

▸ **Survival Brain**

Voice -

- loud, demanding
- sarcastic, patronizing
- whining
- critical, condescending

Body -

- crossed arms, clenched fists
- angry eyes and face
- hands on hips
- rolling your eyes, slamming doors
- inappropriate use of smiling

▸ **Thinking Brain**

Voice -

- clear
- even
- appropriate volume and emphasis

Body -

- open stance
- engaging gestures
- physically at ease
- interested expression

Gender and The Survival Brain

Men and women have some significant differences in terms of how their brains are structured and what chemicals come into play. These differences lead them in very different directions when they downshift into survival brain.

There is a section of our emotional brain, the amygdala, that is part of our scanning system – it tracks on what is occurring around us in support of our brain's primary function, which is to keep us safe.

The amygdala functions differently in men and women. In men, the amygdala is more focused on the external environment and spatial orientation. This helps men negotiate their surroundings (a necessary hunting skill). In women, the amygdala is tuned more toward scanning for emotional information (a necessary nurturing skill).

Another difference is that women (and left-handed men) have brains that are wired to engage both hemispheres simultaneously for all functions except spatial manipulation. (Hence all the multi-tasking.) Right-handed men have thirty percent fewer connecting fibers between the left and right hemispheres in their brain. They are more wired to use one hemisphere at a time, except for spatial manipulation tasks, and then they use both hemispheres simultaneously. (Not surprisingly, right-handed men have a tendency to focus on one thing at a time.)

So, when a right-handed man is in the middle of having strong feelings it can be quite difficult for him to talk about it, because in most people emotions are a right-hemisphere function and language is a left-hemisphere function. (He may be more able to talk about his feelings later, when the stress has passed.)

Under stress, women tend to use more words and are wired to talk, whereas men tend to use fewer words and are wired to act.

Now add oxytocin to the mix. Oxytocin is a brain chemical that promotes the "tend-and-befriend" behaviors. Women have higher levels of oxytocin. Consequently, women often want to connect, focus on feelings, and talk about feelings. For women, the oxytocin plus the cross-hemisphere wiring results in it being much harder for them to disengage from experiencing their emotions in the same way that men can. The bottom line:

Women find safety through relating.

When stressed, women will typically amp up their "tend-and-befriend" behaviors. However, when a stressful moment turns into a complete downshift into survival brain, this need to relate turns into a need to talk, but without self-control. When in survival mode, women are known for "laundry listing" their grievances. Without impulse control, they tend to shame and blame, "guilt-trip" others, and become verbally out of control.

This is very different from how men behave when they downshift into survival gear.

Men find safety by positioning.

Men have higher levels of testosterone, a chemical that contributes to their tendency to compete, be independent, and position. When men downshift into their survival brain, they tend to react in one of three ways:

1. Shut down emotionally

2. Walk away [remove themselves physically]

3. Become physically aggressive

Our default survival brain tendencies are based in our biology, and oftentimes they're culturally reinforced. However, women do not *have* to become emotionally or verbally explosive. Men do not *have* to shut down, leave, or become physically aggressive. These are biological and cultural tendencies, not mandates.

We often get caught up in negatively judging how the other gender handles survival brain moments. We want *them* to behave as *we* would. After all, that's what makes sense – to us.

As your understanding of yourself and others grows, and you integrate the ability to shift yourself out of survival mode, you're likely to notice some significant changes in your ability to engage gender differences respectfully and productively.

Generational Patterns

Notice your survival reaction style. Does it remind you of your parents?

We tend to use whatever fight, flight, or freeze skills our parents used during our first three years of life.

This happens because during those first few years our brains go through some tremendous development processes. The young brain is extremely open, and it is actively building lots of neural connections. The behaviors that are consistently modeled in the environment where a child is being raised form the blueprint for that child's brain development.

Children naturally assume that the way mom and dad (or other primary caregivers) handle life is "the right way" and they wire-in a similar response pattern. A significant portion of the survival brain is wired-up during those first three years.

Your survival brain response is based on what you observed, heard or experienced your mom and dad or other primary caretakers do when they became stressed, upset, or uncomfortable. (Similarly, their survival brain defaults were modeled on what their parents did, and so on.)

Parenting Tip:

You can positively influence your child's survival response.

As a parent, how you react when you are stressed or irritated impacts the survival reactions your child will develop as his or her default.

If you grew up with parents who had a tendency to default to anger, yelling, or overwhelm, you can break the cycle.

As you learn skills to stay calm and competent under duress, you will model healthier strategies for your child.

As your child observes your healthy behaviors, he or she will reformulate their response.

You can give your child the ability to choose healthy responses.

Increase Your Awareness:

- *As a child, what behaviors did you see modeled when your parents (or other primary caregivers) became stressed or upset?*

- *What were they like when they were calm?*

- *How do you behave when you are upset?*

Practice Brain Awareness:

1. Stop and notice. Morning, noon and night – take a moment to stop and notice your attitude and behavior.

2. How would a positive role model stay calm and handle stressful situations?

3. When you are in your thinking brain, how would you describe yourself? What puts you there? How does it feel?

4. What is an early clue that you are starting to get upset?

5. Can you list your top triggers – those moments or situations that "make you mad" or provoke a survival brain response?

6. What responses to stress would you like to model for the important people in your life – your children, colleagues, family, etc.?

Use the spaces below to write the words that describe you when you are operating from your thinking brain and from your survival brain.

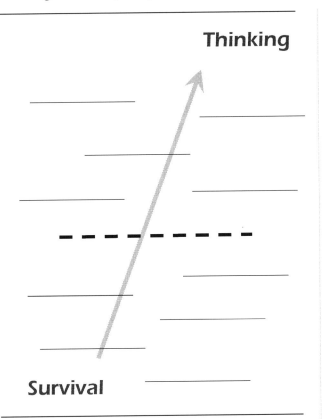

Thinking

Survival

For example . . .

listening
encouraging
patient
flexible
curious
smiling / laughing
sense of humor
calm / relaxed
compassionate
notice what's working

- - - - -

critical / irritable
scared / worried
wanting revenge
screaming
shut down
defensive
withholding
secretive
suspicious

In what scenarios are you most likely to get stuck in your survival brain?

1.

2.

3.

loud noises / voices
upsetting phone calls
heavy traffic
being late
unexpected touch
unwelcome events
money issues
relationship issues
gossip / comparing

Breathing Matters

Breathing Matters
[use your breath to engage your brain]

*Oxygen is the glue
that holds your brain together.*

A human being can live without food for about thirty days, without water for about three days, but we can only last for about three minutes without oxygen. Breathing gives us the oxygen we need to stay alive.

Here's a very quick review of human biology: breathing includes the inhalation of oxygen, which provides your cells with the energy they need, and then exhalation, which facilitates the elimination of toxins. Your red blood cells carry oxygen from your lungs to every cell in your body. That oxygen fuels a variety of automatic processes that keep you healthy and energized. Those processes generate waste-products. Your white blood cells gather up those waste-products (also known as toxins) and carry them to the lining of your lungs. As you exhale, your lungs dispel the toxins. More than half of your toxins are released through exhalation.

For thousands of years people have been engaging breathing practices to achieve and maintain optimal health and performance. Let's explore how and why breathing matters.

Downshifting Into Survival Mode

When a surprise, irritation, or other stress-inducing event occurs, people naturally tend to hold their breath. We call this a startle response.

When you hold your breath, you send a signal to your brain that something is wrong. This signal tells your brain to go into survival mode. During the first eight seconds of holding your breath, you release extra amounts of stress chemicals—including cortisol, norepinephrine, and epinephrine (also known as adrenaline). These chemicals provide an immediate burst of energy, which fuels the fight-or-flight reaction your change in breathing just initiated. When you get started and hold your breath, stress chemicals automatically flood your system and you automatically shift into your survival brain.

As your survival chemicals increase, the chemicals needed to maintain your thinking brain are diminished. There is also a drop in the chemicals needed to maintain your body's health systems – in particular your digestive, immune, and reproductive systems. This is why it's so common to get a headache or a stomach-ache right after a stress trigger.

Did you know?...
Evidence indicates that nine out of ten adults
have impaired breathing patterns.

The Power of Belly Breathing

Conversely, when you slow down and breathe deeply – *into and out from your belly* – your brain gets the message that you're safe. Have you ever experienced a "sigh of relief"?

Here's why belly breathing works: the lower regions of your lungs have larger veins, thus they are able to transfer more oxygen and move it faster into your system. The lower lungs also have more of the nerve receptors that are responsible for sending off the "everything is okay" messages. When you breathe slowly and deeply into your lower lungs (belly breathing) you are triggering more of those calming-message nerve receptors more often, so your brain gets more messages that you are okay. When you hold your breath or engage shallow breathing (using only your upper chest), you trigger more of the upper lung nerve receptors, and those are the receptors that send off the fight-or-flight signals to your brain. This is why people recommend deep breathing, especially if you want to calm down.

Receiving the "all is well" message stops the production of stress chemicals – and it also starts the production of calming chemicals, including serotonin and endorphins. Calming chemicals produce a relaxation response, they promote clear thinking, and they enhance the effectiveness of your body's health systems.

With a shift to belly breathing, you can expect:

- *Improved health*

- *Less anxiety*

- *Lower blood pressure*

- *Clearer thinking*

- *Easier decision making*

- *Consistent effectiveness*

- *More comfortable feelings*

- *More laughter and fun*

- *Increased energy*

- *Greater confidence*

- *Better sleep*

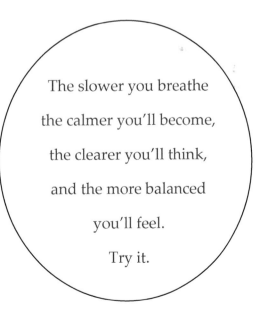

The slower you breathe
the calmer you'll become,
the clearer you'll think,
and the more balanced
you'll feel.

Try it.

The ability

to breathe

well

regardless of

what is

happening

within you

or

around you

will change

your life.

What are the most important times for you to remember to breathe during your day?

❑ First thing in the morning

❑ When you're getting ready for your day

❑ Getting the kids ready for their day

❑ Thinking about your schedule

❑ When you are stuck in traffic

❑ When you get cut off in traffic

❑ When you're interacting with colleagues

❑ When you're late for a meeting

❑ When you are being interrupted

❑ When you're approaching a deadline

❑ When your boss yells at you

❑ When your kids talk back to you

❑ When you're late

❑ When you make a mistake

❑ When nothing is working right

❑ When you're worried, mad, or frustrated

❑ When you can't fall asleep

Belly Breathing: The 2-Minute Fix

To the degree that it's comfortable for you, breathe in and out through your nose. Breathing through your nose helps maintain the correct balance of oxygen and carbon dioxide in your blood, thereby reducing tension and lowering the potential for a "fight-or-flight" response.

- *Sit with your feet about hip-distance apart and flat on the ground. Uncross your arms. Allow your body to be supported by the chair, relax into it, and keep your spine gently straight.*

- *Place one hand on your belly and the other on your chest. Begin by inhaling slowly through your nose, pushing your belly hand away from your spine as you fill your lower lungs with oxygen. Feel your belly hand move out.*

- *Next, slowly release your breath. Empty your upper chest first, then continue exhaling until your belly is empty – the slower the better.*

- *Pause for a moment. Then inhale again – slow, deep, and easy. Feel your belly gently extend.*

- *Again, slowly exhale – longer and slower than you inhaled. Allow your jaw and shoulders to relax a bit more with each exhalation. Pause gently for a moment after each exhale.*

- *Repeat six times, focusing on the steady rise and fall of your hand.*

Remember…

Belly Out

Shoulders Down

Long, Slow Exhalation

When is your breathing effortless?

When do you naturally breathe easily, without any extra attention or effort? In those moments, what are you thinking about? Are you alone or with others? Who are you with? Where are you? What are you doing? Make note of anything that comes to mind.

At Home -

At Work -

Hobbies / Play -

Make your life easier...

People -

Wear clothing that allows you to breathe.

Self-Talk -

Avoid wearing constrictive garments and tight waistbands.

Learn to Breathe in Stressful Environments

Find a place where you can be alone and relax for five minutes. Choose a spot away from your stressful environment.

Practice full belly breathing for five minutes. Try to make your exhalations a little longer than your inhalations. Breathe in for a count of four, and then out for a count of six. Pause for a moment between inhalations and exhalations.

As you breathe, direct your awareness to your counting and the rise and fall of your belly. If distractions occur, redirect your focus back to your counting and to the rise and fall of your belly. Feel your belly move in and out.

Practice this breathing for ten days. Consistent daily practice will benefit you in three ways:

1. You begin to produce a new chemical balance in your body.
2. You develop a heightened awareness of your tension level.
3. You lower your level of acceptable tension. Thus, when you find yourself tensing up, you will find yourself automatically taking a deep breath to reduce the tension.

After ten days, try practicing in your stressful environment. Once or twice each day, practice belly breathing for five full minutes – while remaining engaged in the normal, daily activities of your stressful environment.

The thinking brain doesn't worry.

How slowly and deeply can you breathe when something occurs within you or outside you that you don't like?

Practice Breathing:

Breathe to Reduce Stress

- When you notice you have body tension or stress, simply lengthen and emphasize your exhalation. A slow, focused exhalation turns on your parasympathetic nervous system, which activates your relaxation response.

- Continue to breathe slowly until your hands are warm and you feel relaxed.

Breathe While Driving

- Sit so that both sides of your bottom are evenly supported.

- Relax your shoulders.

- Become aware of your hands, and allow your fingers to relax as you hold the wheel.

- As you inhale, focus on expanding your belly out, slowly. Feel your belly button move away from your spine while your lower back presses against the car seat.

- Exhale slowly. *Engage your abdomen for a full exhalation.* Completely empty your belly.

- Repeat five times.

- Notice how you feel.

Breathe to Remain Professional

When a surprise happens at work and you need to stay professional...

- Before saying or doing anything, take two deep breaths.

- Imagine yourself handling the situation well. Envision yourself remaining calm and clear, and communicating easily.

- If you notice that you or others are becoming a bit reactive, take several long, slow, deep breaths.

Remember, your ability to breathe well and remain calm will affect other people's ability to breathe well and remain calm. *Your breathing has an influence on both the dynamic and the outcome.*

Deepen Your Breathing

- Place one hand on your belly and the other on your lower back.
- As you inhale, feel both hands move out, away from each other.
- As you exhale, feel them move in toward each other.
- Repeat a few times, and notice how you feel.

Really Good Times to Breathe...

▶ When you lie down in bed at night

▶ Before you get up in the morning *(empty your lungs of last night's air)*

▶ Before you eat *(breathing turns on your digestive system)*

▶ Before you greet *(over the phone or in person)*

▶ When you encounter a sudden change or surprise

▶ When you are with someone who is frightened or angry

Do a Mental Rehearsal:

You probably already know that visualizing is often recommended as a self-development tool. In fact, it's one of your most effective tools. Here's why:

Your brain cannot tell the difference between a real and a vividly imagined situation.

When you run through a mental rehearsal, your brain integrates the experience, as you imagine it, as if you had actually done it! Strong visualization plus fully engaged breathing will significantly accelerate your learning and skill integration. This is why top performers use this practice, regularly. It's well worth your time.

- Identify a situation in which you would like to remain calmer, and start deep breathing.

- Visualize yourself in the situation. See yourself feeling calm and controlled... breathing slowly... deeply... easily...

- Repeat three or four times.

- Stay with it until you can breathe in and out slowly, deeply, and easily.

- When you can imagine the situation and achieve a full, deep exhalation at the same time, it indicates that you have integrated your new skill.

Parenting Tip:

Use your breathing to calm your child's difficult moments. When you are breathing fully and easily, you can parent consistently and calmly.

Children match their parent's breathing. How you breathe will determine how your child breathes.

Children follow your example. They adjust their breathing (unconsciously) to match yours. When you want to help your children calm down, slow and deepen *your* breathing.

The slower you breathe the calmer you will become. With just two minutes of slow, deep breathing your breathing pattern will impact your children's breathing and they will begin to calm down.

When your child comes to you to talk about her upset – maybe she just fell down, or she got into a fight at school, or her feelings are hurt, or perhaps she's mad at you – it is *your* slow, deep breathing during her moment of upset that will give her a sense of calm and safety.

When you slow down and breathe easily during an upset, you teach children that life is manageable.

SHIFTING GEARS: A BRAIN-BASED APPROACH TO ENGAGING YOUR BEST SELF

Self-Talk Tune-up

Self-Talk Tune-up
[listen to what you're saying]

*What you say to yourself in
the first few seconds after a surprise,
stress, or irritation occurs determines whether
you stay in your thinking brain or
downshift into your survival brain.*

Evidence suggests that we can have up to 60,000 self-talk moments a day, and each thought has an immediate impact on our physiology. Now remember, your brain cannot tell the difference between a real and a vividly imagined event – so just thinking a fear-based thought signals your brain that danger exists. And then there you go, into survival brain! Then what happens? Poor thinking, headaches and stomachaches.

Think about something that you feel calm or confident about. Notice how your breathing and physiology are different than when you think about something that triggers angry or defensive feelings. Research indicates that up to 98% of some people's thinking is focused on what they *don't* like and *don't* want. We tend to focus on judgments, resentments, and disappointments… and as a result we feel angry, worried, tired, and overwhelmed.

To change how you feel, change the focus of your thinking.

---→

What you think about, you bring about.

When a challenge occurs and you say to yourself *"It's okay... I can handle this...."* your brain perceives competence, and you remain in your thinking brain.

However, when you think *"This is awful!"* you create insecurity, which sends out a fear alert. Your brain responds by preparing a defensive reaction. Suddenly you downshift into your survival brain – and you no longer have access to your thinking brain. *Survival brain skills and thinking brain skills are mutually exclusive – you can access one skill set or the other, but not both at the same time.* So, when you downshift into survival mode, it is *literally* impossible to access your thinking brain skills – compassion, creativity, collaboration, problem solving, etc.

No wonder we feel overwhelmed when we go into survival mode. The survival brain cannot generate options or find solutions - that is not it's job. Now if you need to run really fast or pick up an impossibly heavy object, the survival brain is the best gear to be in. But if you need to think, relate to someone, or come up with a solution, it's really not so useful.

⟶ *The words you choose and use*

will shift you

into your thinking brain

or into your survival brain.

Notice what you're saying. *When you are headed in an unwanted direction, shift gears.* To stay in your thinking brain, go for the internal dialogue and the outwardly spoken words that create the attitude and outcomes you want.

Engage Productive Self-Talk:

Relax… It's okay…

I can deal with this…

I'll figure it out… We'll figure it out…

Yes, it's uncomfortable… and I can manage…

I can choose what to focus on…

I can be my best, even now…

Something good can come of this…

I have faith this will work out…

What am I learning? What are we learning?

I can find the humor here… It's kind of funny…

I can feel myself calming down…

I can hear myself think…

I'm strong… I can deal with this…

I'm in control of myself…

I'm bigger than this… We're bigger than this…

I trust myself…

I can choose…

I can be generous right now…

I hear my voice calming down…

I can steady myself…

We can work with this…

We'll see our way through this…

I have the ability to handle this…

What do I want to model to my kids right now?

I can be patient in this moment…

Good time to count to ten… or 100…

Time out… I'm taking a walk…

I'm letting this go - it's not worth the toxins…

This too shall pass…

Want to get to your thinking brain quickly?

Many people have found success using this self-talk statement:

I love and accept myself exactly as I am right now.

This message cuts to the core of personal distress for many people.

Try it. See if it's a fit for you.

Avoid Negatives

When constructing your self-talk and your dialogue with others, focus on what you do want rather than what you don't want. Why? Try this: Don't think about standing up right now. What did you just imagine? Bet it was standing up.

Why? Once again, it has to do with brain wiring. **Your brain does not process negatives.** Instead, it produces an image or feeling about what you tell it to avoid. So when you use negative phrasing it inadvertently sends your brain a message to focus on what you're trying to avoid. Even though your intention is quite the opposite.

Replace what you *don't want* with a request for what you *do want*. For example, *"I'm not going to yell at Billy"* could be rephrased as *"I'll stay calm when I talk with Billy."*

Pointing out what you don't want is a form of blaming or complaining, whereas asking for the new behavior you do want invites a more thinking brain interaction. *Try asking directly for what you DO want – and be specific.*

Notice your phrasing, both in your self-talk and in your conversations with others. Try replacing *"I don't _____"* thoughts and conversations with *"I do _____"* messages. Just play around with it, and see what kind of results you get.

*Just Trying
To Help...*

Negative phrasing is so ingrained in our culture that we often use it without ever realizing it. We even use negatives when we're trying to be helpful. Try playing with rephrasing your well-intended messages...

Don't worry.
› **It'll work out.**

Don't mention it.
› **You're welcome.**

I wouldn't leave you high and dry.
› **I'm here for you.**

No objections.
› **Works for me.**

No worries.
› **It's okay.**

Parenting Tip:

 What you say when you are stressed becomes your child's internal dialogue.

When an upset occurs at home, try using solution-focused language to help your family stay resourceful and resilient.

Choose empowering thoughts and words. Say them *out loud* – especially when you're stressed.

Find positive statements that feel right for you. Be a model for choosing thinking and language that is constructive and productive.

Remember, your internal dialogue replicates what your parents said under stress. You can change the model for your child.

Here are a couple of possibilities:

- *"We might not like what just happened, but we're really good at coming up with solutions. We're going to work this out."*

- *"We'll get through this. We can do this."*

It may feel a bit odd at first, but think about the benefits: you can help your child develop their self-confidence and positive self-talk skills.

→ **You can't always control your first thought, but you CAN choose your second thought, and you CAN choose your response.**

Remember – you have eight seconds until your survival brain chemicals fully kick into gear.

And if you stop and think about it, **eight seconds is a long time!**

You DO have enough time to choose a thought that calms you, relaxes you, and that leads you toward creating a successful outcome. Eight seconds is plenty of time to change your mind.

Sally and Joe are having a great weekend. And they're going to take the kids to the zoo this afternoon. Sally walks in and informs Joe that she's invited her mom to come along.

"Oh, no..." Joe thinks, "Jane is always late. If we wait for her to show up, there's no way we'll see everything, let alone get back in time for a barbeque." Joe feels his heat rising, and as he opens his mouth to protest, he stops. He takes a few deep breaths, and tells himself, "I don't want to go there. I know Sally loves her mom and she's been looking for ways to include her more. And Jane is lots of fun... once she shows up. What can I do here?" He gives it a minute, till he's breathing easily again. Then he says, "Hey Sally, any way we could make sure to leave by 2:00? I want to have plenty of time to get there and look around without feeling rushed in this heat. Could we ask your mom to get here early? Or maybe she could be ready to go and we'll pick her up on the way? What do you think?"

Moods Are Contagious

One "downer" person can affect the mood of the whole group, and so can one "up-beat" person.

Ever wonder why that's so? It's because most of the systems in your body are closed-loop, which means they self-manage and self-regulate, but the limbic system is different. The limbic system (your emotional center) is an open-loop system that depends primarily on external sources to regulate and manage itself. Our limbic systems are impacted by the emotions of others. In fact, both positive and negative emotions can spread between people and among a group, in much the same way that a cold can.

The process wherein a person consciously or unconsciously influences the emotions of others is called emotional contagion. We've all experienced the phenomena in a number of different ways. Can you recall a time when you were in a group, and someone entered the room and suddenly everyone got tense? Or maybe just the opposite, where someone walked in and suddenly the mood lightened and people started smiling. Or perhaps you've been in a situation where you're part of a group that is pretty well-bonded, and you've felt the awkwardness when someone new tries to join in late in the game.

If you're around a lot of negative people, or a really negative person that you are greatly impacted by, it is essential that you develop and maintain a strong emotional immune system.

The words we use can help us (and others) to stay in our thinking brain, or they can serve as a negative trigger.

Avoid these words...

These words cause people to hold their breath, which shifts them into survival brain. Try to avoid using them – with yourself or others.

Notice what you're saying...

When you open your mouth, do you bring people up, or do you break them down?

You or I ...

- *should*
- *can't*
- *won't*
- *didn't*
- *always*
- *never*

You are / I am ...

- *a loser*
- *stupid*
- *lame*
- *weak*

The use of language that limits, demeans or criticizes shifts everyone, speaker and listeners alike, down into their survival brain.

Stop engaging in conversations that trigger the survival brain...

Do the conversations you're in help you and others to heal, or do they expand the pain?

- *Shaming, blaming, complaining*
- *Criticizing*
- *Comparing*
- *Personalizing*
- *Recycling disappointments*
- *Energizing the drama*

- *Repeating stories of woe: "Poor me" or "Poor Joe"*
- *"Ain't it awful!"*
- *Put-downs and snide remarks*
- *Gossip*
- *Whining*
- *Angry outbursts*

Instead, try to redirect your conversations towards...

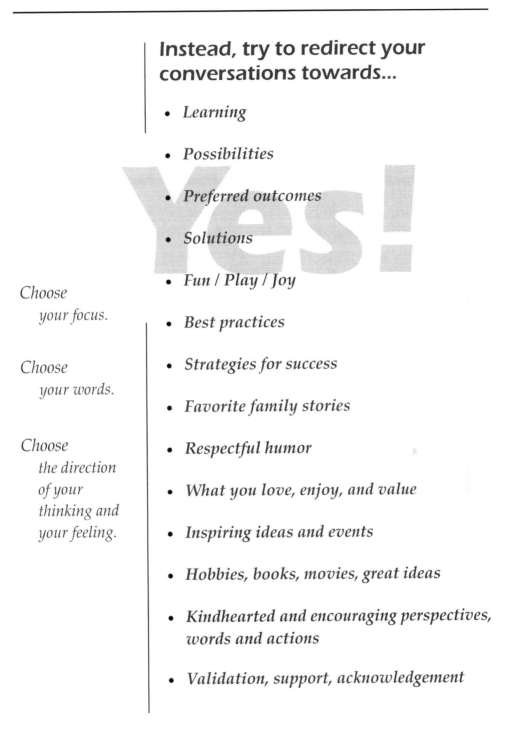

- *Learning*

- *Possibilities*

- *Preferred outcomes*

- *Solutions*

- *Fun / Play / Joy*

- *Best practices*

- *Strategies for success*

- *Favorite family stories*

- *Respectful humor*

- *What you love, enjoy, and value*

- *Inspiring ideas and events*

- *Hobbies, books, movies, great ideas*

- *Kindhearted and encouraging perspectives, words and actions*

- *Validation, support, acknowledgement*

*Choose
   your focus.*

*Choose
   your words.*

*Choose
   the direction
   of your
   thinking and
   your feeling.*

Parenting Tip:

 Foster your child's resilience.

Mistakes + Reflection = Learning

We learn from mistakes – our own or others. However, this can present a bit of a quandary, because we live in a culture that is biased against making mistakes. We think we need to get it right, the first time.

A more useful orientation is to understand that learning occurs when we've made a mistake and then reflect on how we'd do it differently next time.

A "mistake" is actually just a practice moment linked with a critical judgment. For instance, when we learned how to read, write, and figure out math equations we probably made plenty of mistakes. When we're learning, we expect to make mistakes. We understand that we're learning, we call it practice, and *we don't judge it.* We value the mistake as a normal part of the learning process.

Learning from a mistake while maintaining a positive sense of self helps develop resilience. Resilience is essential for lifelong well-being. It is developed or diminished by what we say to ourselves as soon as we make a mistake.

The ability to learn from a mistake is determined by what we say to ourselves right after the mistake moment occurs. If children learn to say *"I can figure this out"* they will hang in there, develop resilience, and grow an empowered learning attitude. Their thinking brain will remain engaged, and as a result they *can* figure it out.

When children develop their ability to be comfortable with "making practice," they also develop self-confidence and self-esteem.

If children say *"I'm so stupid!"* or if they hear others say *"What a loser!"* after they've made a mistake, their survival brain kicks into gear, and that prevents them from being able to learn from the moment. In survival mode, they can't accurately assess the situation and/or find the solutions. They literally cannot figure it out, because they are not in the portion of their brain that *can* think and figure things out. Thus, they often will repeat the mistake, sometimes over and over again.

What you say to yourself or to your child when either of you makes a mistake shapes your child's lifelong resilience.

Increase Your Awareness:

- *What are some of your common negative self-talk statements?*

- *What self-talk statements would you like to use consistently?*

- *In what situations would you like to experience more confidence? What self-talk would generate that confidence for you?*

Practice Choosing Your Response:

What do you say to yourself when you feel overwhelmed or frustrated? What would you like to say instead?

Old:
New:

What do you say to yourself when your child talks back to you? What would you like to say instead?

Old:
New:

What do you say / think when another driver cuts you off? What would you like to say / think instead?

Old:
New:

What do you say when a colleague acts disrespectfully? What would you like to say instead?

Old:
New:

Parenting Tip:

▶ *Direct the dialogue at the dinner table.*

Notice the conversation when you gather with others to eat. Listen to both tone and content. Try to engage in upbeat, positive conversations at the dinner table.

If the conversation becomes negative, play with engaging in a manner that redirects the focus. You might try steering the conversation toward talking about what you love, things you are looking forward to, or what you're enjoying. Talk about highlights of the day, what went well, what you learned, and how you solved problems.

Why? Well, once again... it's all about biology. Remember, if you subject yourself to negative or critical conversations while eating, your survival brain kicks into gear. When your survival brain is engaged, your digestive system is compromised – and so is everyone else's at the table. This results in upset stomachs, reduced self-esteem, and even fat retention. (*Now how's that for motivation!*)

Practice Productive Self-Talk:

1. Begin each morning by creating a picture of your day unfolding exactly as you would like. Take one minute and imagine what you are like when you are at your best, your happiest, your healthiest, your most successful.

2. Take a moment at least twice a day to stop and see yourself as happy, confident and effective. Get the feeling of what that is like for you. Feel that feeling for at least ten seconds.

3. Find another person who also wants to practice staying in high-quality, thinking brain conversations. Start with ten minutes. During that time, talk about anything you love, what you are looking forward to, what you'd like to see happen, books and movies you enjoy, qualities you admire in other people, what's going well in your life, or activities you enjoy.

4. Notice the focus of your conversations with your best friends. Can you turn a conversation around? See if you can influence the direction of a complaining conversation into one that is helpful, humorous, or productive. Are you talking about satisfying things you are wanting to create, or complaining about something or someone? When women gather they have a tendency to talk about their complaints and

disappointments (survival brain), whereas men tend to talk about activities. See if you can include some positive solutions when the conversation turns toward blaming, shaming, or complaining.

5. Can you hold your tongue if the conversation turns to gossip? Can you stop yourself from engaging? Instead, you could try to add value… maybe point out something you appreciate about the person being scrutinized, or perhaps just remove yourself from that conversation.

6. Can you have an uncomfortable feeling and remain in your thinking brain at the same time? The next time you feel disappointed, sad, or confused, can you also identify something that you appreciate about yourself, your life, or your day? *(Hint: breathing helps.)*

7. Write in a journal for a few minutes each day. Write about what you love, what you want, what brings you joy, what you desire, your goals and dreams. Identify obstacles that stand in the way of you achieving what you want. Identify what steps you can take to overcome these obstacles.

8. Look at the clock for eight seconds. As you are doing so, notice how many thoughts you can have in that amount of time. In eight

seconds you can imagine tremendous success, or you can envision doom and gloom. You could create a desired outcome, or you can wreck your day, in just eight seconds. Where does your brain go?

9. Do a mental rehearsal:

- Identify a situation in which you would like to use more positive self-talk statements.

- Choose the self-talk statements you would like to be using. (For example, *"I can handle this…"* or *"I'll figure this out…."*)

- Use your imagination. See yourself in the situation, using your new internal dialogue, being calm and self-controlled.

- Repeat three or four times.

- Stay with it until you can breathe in and out slowly, deeply, and easily.

- When you can imagine this situation and achieve a full, deep exhalation at the same time, it indicates that you have integrated your new skill.

The Importance of Telling Yourself The Truth

> ▸ *Telling yourself the truth*
> *is profoundly empowering.*

> ▸ *Telling yourself the truth*
> *activates your thinking brain.*

> ▸ *Telling yourself the truth*
> *is essential for well-being.*

Unfortunately, many of us are quite familiar with telling ourselves *un*-truths. We might be afraid our truth would not be acceptable to others. We say yes when we really want to say no. We say we're fine when really we're feeling sad. We pretend. We avoid. We lie to ourselves about what we're feeling, what we want, what we need, what we're thinking. We try to talk ourselves into what we think we *should* and *ought to* do or be or have. We don't own up to what is really so for us.

However, your body always knows what's true and what's not true. You can fool your mind (in fact, your mind is often the last to know), but you cannot fool your body. Your body is deeply instinctual, naturally. *Your body knows what is so.*

When you tell yourself anything other than your truth, you send your system a message that it's not safe to tell the truth. Your brain reads this as a threat, it goes into defensive mode, and your survival brain is triggered.

One way out of this spiral is to stop, breathe, and take a moment to get honest with yourself.

- *What is your honest emotion in this moment?*
- *What do you truly want for yourself right now?*

In your mind (or in your journal) fill in the blanks: *I feel _____ and I want _____.*

Telling yourself the truth strengthens your body. Telling yourself anything other than the truth literally weakens your body.

Allow your truth. When you tell yourself the truth you will instantly release the grip of your survival brain.

It kind of gives a whole new meaning to that old saying, *"The truth shall set you free."*

Repair Relationships

Repair Relationships
[remap your future]

Often as people learn about how their brain works, they look back upon their past behaviors and recognize that they have reacted from their survival brain with people they love. They want to go back and undo the damage these behaviors might have caused. One way to do this is to go to the person and apologize for those earlier behaviors.

Going back and cleaning up is particularly important with children. The behaviors and reactions we modeled, especially when our children were quite young, become wired into their brains as "the right way" to handle life's scenarios and stressors. Just as we tell ourselves that *we* don't want to do what *our* parents did (and then we surprise ourselves when we catch it happening), our children could easily find themselves replicating our survival brain reactions. Unless we break that cycle.

Our apologies can change intergenerational patterns of reacting with anger.

We build trust as we learn to treat one another respectfully at all times – whether we agree or disagree, regardless of what mood we're in or the prevailing feeling in the moment.

Most of us have not known *how* to shift out of our survival brain. So when we felt upset or at odds with somebody (which most of us have had plenty of practice with) we changed our behavior in some way that occurred to the other person as disagreeable or offensive. This tends to diminish trust in the relationship, as the other person learns that we'll only treat them respectfully when they agree with us.

As we learn and use the skills that keep us in our thinking brain, we learn we can have a variety of opinions and conversations with others in calm and respectful ways.

We can disagree without being disagreeable.

The approach to apologizing outlined here is a bit different from most other approaches.

Typically, people think an apology consists of saying *"I'm sorry and I won't ever do that again."* And in the moment they say it, they really mean it. But when the same scenario occurs a few weeks later, and the same behavior is repeated (as is so often the case) that apology becomes meaningless.

What's the alternative?

Game-Changing Apologies

1. Go to the person whom you want to give your apology to and ask them if they have a moment to receive an apology from you. If it's not a good time for them, find a time that works for both of you.

2. Describe the situation and your behavior that you are apologizing for.

3. Tell the person you genuinely apologize for what you did.

4. Now tell them how you wish had handled it, or how you intend to handle any similar moments in the future.

5. Listen to what they need to say, if anything, in response – and accept their words. Allow yourself to hear and receive this feedback. Refrain from minimizing their experience or engaging a debate in any way.

6. Thank them for being willing to hear your apology, and then express your appreciation for the relationship.

What makes this approach to apologizing different is that fourth step. When you take a moment to think about how you would handle that situation better, you create a scenario in your brain that becomes a sort of template for success. Since your brain doesn't know the difference between a real and an imagined thought, you now have a new way to handle yourself in that situation. When you tell the other person how you wish you had handled it, or how you intend to handle any similar moments in the future, both of you are engaging new skills – and you are increasing the likelihood that you will remember those new skills. This is how you replace old behaviors with new ones.

Some people hesitate to make apologies because it can be uncomfortable – and it certainly can be. Many people think that

Remapping your response is the critical link that builds trust and alters destructive behavioral patterns.

apologizing puts them in a vulnerable, "one-down" position. This is one of the reasons why apologizing tends to be more challenging for men than for women. In fact, women tend to apologize for actions or situations that they are not even responsible for.

When you take responsibility for your past survival brain behaviors, you can begin to rebuild trust. Your willingness to authentically apologize for painful past behaviors and tell others how you will handle yourself in the future will dramatically change your relationships. Here's an example. Joe is talking with his daughter, Mandy:

Mandy, got a minute? I want to apologize for something.

Sure, I guess so.

You know the other night when I walked into your room and yelled at you to turn your music down? I apologize. I shouldn't have barged in without knocking, and I'm sorry that I yelled at you. I've been thinking about it. I wish I'd waited till I had calmed down, and then just knocked on your door – and waited for you to answer. Then I could have just asked you to turn it down, without blasting you.

Okay. Thanks for telling me.

I love you kiddo.

Love you, too.

Some Useful Guidelines About Apologizing

- Offer apologies only when they are heartfelt and genuine. It's empowering for both you and the other person involved when you apologize because you want a better relationship or you want to heal the relationship. Apologize because you want to, not because you think you should or have to – these are survival brain reactions.

- When apologizing, steer clear of defending or justifying your behavior.

- Refrain from demanding or expecting others to forgive you.

- Don't expect an immediate feel-good response from others. Remember, you are apologizing to make *your* amends, not to get something *from* the other person.

- Please remember that apologies that actually mean something cannot be extracted. You can offer an apology, but refrain from demanding one. If you have a need to control or dictate someone else's behavior, it suggests that you have downshifted into your survival brain. It's a red flag that you're operating under a false premise – that somebody else determines your feelings, and that they "owe it to you" to fix your feelings. You may want to review the *Feel Your Feelings* chapter and use the strategies listed there to manage yourself when your uncomfortable feelings arise.

- If you are apologizing to children, make it age appropriate.

- Be aware that if apologizing is new behavior on your part, the people you are apologizing to might feel threatened, surprised or suspicious about your efforts. Understand that they are entitled to extend or withhold trust as they deem right for their sense of safety. While their hesitancy may feel a bit uncomfortable for you, remember that you can manage your uncomfortable feelings without taking their responses personally. If you notice you're encountering resistance, you can still proceed forward – respectfully and authentically. As others see you being consistent and sincere in your commitment to change, they may feel more space to breathe easily, relax, and learn to trust you. Be aware that it may take time. Be patient, and be at peace with the only person you can control – yourself.

Increase Your Awareness:

What was your model of apologizing growing up?

_____

_____

_____

_____

_____

_____

When is it easy to apologize now, and to whom?

_____

_____

_____

_____

_____

_____

_____

_____

_____

_____

When have you received an apology that has healed a rift in a relationship? What are some examples of apologies you have received that have been healing, meaningful, or impactful for you?

_____

_____

_____

_____

_____

_____

Are there any people or situations in your life where you think you may owe or want to extend an apology, but you imagine it would be too uncomfortable? What would it cost you and what might you gain to extend that apology? What fear could be holding you back?

_____

_____

_____

_____

_____

_____

Practice Your Apologies:

1. Start simply, with a trusted friend.

Identify an apology you would like to extend to someone who is a trusted friend. Pick someone who is easy for you to interact with. Practice the six steps of a game-changing apology with that person.

2. Do a mental rehearsal.

- Identify a situation or behavior in which you would like to offer an apology. Pick one that feels somewhat challenging.

- Think through the steps of this new apology process and what you would like to say to this person (or these people). If it helps you clarify your thinking, write it out.

- In your imagination, see yourself offering your apology to the person or people you have in mind. See yourself feeling calm, authentic, and easily exercising self-control.

- Repeat three or four times.

- Stay with it until you can breathe in and out slowly, deeply, and easily.

- When you can imagine this situation and achieve a full, deep exhalation at the same time, it indicates that you have integrated your new skill.

Feel Your Feelings

Feel Your Feelings
[but act from your values]

Feelings change moment to moment.
Values are enduring.

The nature of feelings is that they change, often. Because your emotions are connected to your thinking, with every new thought you might have a new feeling. Given that we have as many as 60,000 thoughts a day, it's likely that you can go through a lot of feelings on any given day.

Values tend to be more enduring. While they certainly can and do evolve, in general they remain fairly constant. Everyone has values; they reflect our current ideas of our best selves.

In this chapter we'll explore feelings and values in some depth. You'll notice that they are quite different, yet we often mix them up. (And we also mix up feelings and behaviors – we'll sort that out as well.)

Here's the bottom line: feelings are a great tool for navigating the immediate moment. Values help you set and adjust course in the bigger picture. Having some clarity about how feelings and values operate will significantly aid you in bringing your best self forward.

Feel Your Feelings...

Feelings play a very important role. They are your body's way of telling you that you like or don't like what you are experiencing in any given moment.

Feelings connect you with yourself and with the present moment.

Feelings are your built-in feedback system. They let you know if your thoughts and actions are moving you closer to or further away from what you want.

You create each feeling you have.

Did you know that? It's new information for a lot of people. But it's true: you create your own feelings. In fact other people do not (indeed they cannot) "make you" feel anything.

Creating a feeling is a simple 3-step process:

1. Some stimulus or event occurs.

2. You tell yourself a story about it.

3. That story creates a feeling.

Here are a couple of examples:

Some stimulus or event occurs:	*The new dog makes a mess on your carpet.*
You tell yourself a story about it:	*"Oh, no! This is terrible! The carpet is wrecked! That smell is never gonna come out. Agh!! Why in the world did I agree to getting a dog?! What was I thinking?!!"*
That story creates a feeling:	*Anger, frustration, tension*

Same stimulus/event, *different emotion…*

Some stimulus or event occurs:	*The new dog makes a mess on your carpet.*
You tell yourself a story about it:	*"Oh boy…That's gonna take some cleaning up. Hmm… looks like we're gonna need to work on training. Good to know. Well, guess I get to try out that new miracle cleaner sooner than later. I hope it works – I sure could use a miracle today…"*
That story creates a feeling:	*Competence, confidence, humor*

Scenario #2:

Some stimulus or event occurs:	*Your coworker, Charlie, publicly slams your idea.*
You tell yourself a story about it:	*"Unbelievable!! You #%*$!!! I bet you didn't even read my report. Of course it'll work. Anyone with half a brain could see that! That guy just can't stand anyone else having the good idea."*
That story creates a feeling:	*Anger, resentment, tension, anxiety*

Same stimulus/event, ***different emotion…***

Some stimulus or event occurs:	*Your coworker, Charlie, publicly slams your idea.*
You tell yourself a story about it:	*"Huh, that's unusual… I wonder what's up with Charlie…usually he talks with me privately if he's got questions or concerns. Hmm… Well, if there's time we'll hash it out now. If not, I'll catch him between meetings and work it out…"*
That story creates a feeling:	*Empathy, curiosity, concern, collaboration*

No one makes you feel angry, mad, or sad.

Do you ever find yourself thinking or saying something like "_____ *makes me so mad!!!*"? The idea that anybody else (or something outside of you) can make you feel anything is very well ingrained in our culture. But that doesn't make it accurate.

You choose what you say to yourself. *You* choose the story you tell yourself, and as a result *you* choose the feelings you have.

You create your own feelings by how you interpret events. The stories you tell yourself about the event (your self-talk) set the tone and direction of your emotional response. Change your self-talk and you'll change your feelings.

Feelings help you navigate.

Feelings are kind of like radar – they help you know where you are in the present moment.

Being aware of what you're feeling helps you make good choices. Feelings let you know how you're doing relative to where you want to be headed. If you need to make a change to correct course you can activate your thinking brain and make the appropriate adjustments.

Being cut off from your feelings is kind of like navigating without radar.

Many people have the idea that having feelings is weak or irrational. They are not used to allowing and actually *feeling* their feelings. As a result, they have a tendency to become rather uncomfortable when feelings occur. It can feel very much like something is wrong or that they are losing control. You may recognize this discomfort as anxiety, insecurity, or anger.

The thing is that we, as human beings, *do* have feelings. We can't *not* have them. We all have feelings, all day long, every day.

We have both physical feelings and emotional feelings. Physical feelings are your body's way of giving you feedback about your physical state – you're hot, cold, tired, hungry, sleepy, etc. Physical feelings tell you what you need physically. You also have emotional feelings – you're happy, excited, overwhelmed, insecure, anxious, etc. Emotional feelings tell you what you need mentally and behaviorally. The focus of this chapter is emotional feelings.

Every time you engage your internal dialogue, you generate an emotional feeling or range of feelings. When you notice some event or something crosses your mind, you tell yourself a story about it, and you have a feeling that associates with that story. You might label it "a happy thought" or perhaps "a disturbing idea." Whatever the content, the process is the same.

We are, by nature, feeling beings. Feelings are an inherent and necessary part of our structure. Feelings give us critical feedback. They help us navigate through our moments, days, and lives.

When you have an uncomfortable feeling that surfaces regularly, it is your body's way of telling you that you have an important need that's not being met. Use this feeling to discover what's out of balance and to explore what actions you can take to restore the balance.

All feelings are valuable.

There is no such thing as a "good feeling" or a "bad feeling." There are certainly more and less comfortable feelings, but comfortable does not equal "better" or "right." Every feeling contains valuable information.

Feelings exist, and our job is to feel them and learn from them. Not to judge them. Not to fix them. Just feel them and learn from them.

Families can have emotional rules. It's not unusual to have grown up in a family that was uncomfortable with certain feelings. In some families it's not okay to be angry, or to show fear, or to be proud of your accomplishments. These rules can be unintended, they're usually unspoken, and quite often they're unconscious. But they can influence us a lot, even in our adult lives.

For example, anger is a healthy feeling, one that children normally experience toward parents, friends, and classmates. If you grew up in a family that didn't allow children to feel angry at their parents, you may find yourself feeling quite uncomfortable when your child freely expresses anger toward you. Looking back, you might see how your parents had emotional rules that were set up in their childhood, which were in turn influenced by the rules their parents grew up with, and so on. You are the current link in a lineage of rules and patterns.

If you find yourselves operating within a set of rules that include a tendency to judge or disallow certain emotions, it greatly behooves you to question those rules. While it's certainly true that some feelings are more comfortable than others, *all* feelings are legitimate.

You have the right to your feelings – and so does everyone else.

We all have the right to our feelings, whatever they may be. Your feelings do not need to match or agree with anybody else's feelings, and often they won't. You do not need anyone else's approval to have your feelings, and others do not need your approval or agreement to legitimize their feelings.

Each and every one of us is entitled to feel whatever we feel. We don't need permission to have our feelings.

Feelings and actions are different.

When you are having a strong feeling, don't act.

A major mistake that people often make is to act impulsively when they have strong and/or uncomfortable feelings. It's good to remember that when it comes to actions, our job is to *choose* them. It is critical to feel and learn from our feelings, but *only* act from our values.

For example, you can *feel* really angry and still *choose behaviors* that are respectful. You really can engage personal management strategies that steer clear of behaving in an angry, violent or disrespectful manner. In fact, the *need* to act when you're having an intense feeling (positive or negative) is an indication that you are not using impulse control. (There is more about impulse control later on in this chapter.)

Feelings and thoughts are different.

People also confuse feelings and thoughts, and they're not the same thing. When we are thinking, we are either focusing on the *future* (projecting) or reviewing the *past* (reflecting). We cannot think about the *present* moment, because in the time in takes to think about it, that moment has passed.

We experience *the present moment* in three ways:

1. Conscious breathing (*intentional*)
2. Feeling feelings (*emotions*)
3. Feeling body sensations *(hot, cold, tired, etc.)*

Do you notice how all three require you to be "present" in your body?

> *You have to be in your body*
> *to be in the present moment.*

Try this: think about this moment. Notice how as soon as you start to think about the present moment, it passes. The present can become the past, quickly. Now feel this moment – notice how your fingers feel, or what emotions you are having. As long as you stay connected to what you are *feeling*, even though the feelings might change, you stay in the present moment.

Have you ever noticed how common it is for people to ask *"How are you?"* when they meet? This greeting is essentially asking *"How are you feeling?"* Oftentimes people will give an automatic reply, usually something like *"Fine. You?"* But sometimes we actually stop, maybe just for a moment, and *feel* the present moment. We check in with ourselves, and then we share our information – we might say, *"I'm so excited."* or *"I'm kind of confused."* or maybe we just offer up a simple summary, *"I'm good."*

Feelings provide you with information from your emotional realm. They tell you how you're doing in any given moment, and where you are in relation to what you desire. Feelings help you navigate toward your goals and dreams. That's why people who are disconnected or disengaged from their feelings are *literally* disempowered – they are missing a primary feedback system.

Thoughts, on the other hand, are the way you engage your mental realm. Thoughts include all your ideas, opinions, creative inspirations, options, strategies, and so forth.

You'll hear people use the words *"I feel"* before stating a thought. For example, *"I feel you're getting too worked up about this."* This is a thought. More distinctly, it's an opinion. The feeling might be annoyed, as in *"I feel annoyed that you're so worked up about this."* Or it might be frustrated, as in *"I feel frustrated that you're so worked up about this."*

When the word after *"feel"* is an emotion *(happy, sad, frustrated, anxious, etc.)* you are expressing a feeling. When *"feel"* is followed by either *"you"* or *"that"* you are expressing a thought or belief (and quite often it's a judgment or projection).

Of course, it's fine to have your thoughts – whatever they may be. *"I feel you should have gotten here on time."* or *"I feel that's too much to pay."* Both are completely valid thoughts. But, please notice: these are thoughts, not feelings. The feeling correlates might be *"I feel frustrated that you're late."* or *"I feel uncomfortable paying that much."*

It's quite common to mix up the expression of thoughts and feelings. But it's better not to. Try to clarify your language, so that everyone (you included) can have a better understanding of whatever it is you're trying to say.

How do you want to feel on a regular basis?

Safe	Peaceful
Secure	Curious
Relaxed	Confident
Refreshed	Satisfied
Engaged	Amused
Inspired	Loving
Excited	Compassionate
Energetic	Comfortable
Optimistic	Clear-headed
Appreciative	Calm
Grateful	Happy
Passionate	*(There are plenty more… add your own…)*

How do you feel right now?

Happy	Grateful
Sad	Pleased
Mad	Refreshed
Glad	Daring
Concerned	Worthy
Confused	Wanted
Anxious	Upset
Satisfied	Elated
Content	Relieved
Amused	Humiliated
Excited	Irritated
Embarrassed	Joyful
Frightened	Abandoned
Hurt	Eager
Disappointed	Delighted
Angry	Invigorated
Scared	Curious
Worried	Calm
Guilty	Gentle
Grumpy	*(There are plenty more… add your own…)*

What feelings hold you hostage?

Feelings generally fall into two categories – comfortable and uncomfortable. We love our comfortable feelings. It's the uncomfortable feelings we have issues with.

The fear of feeling uncomfortable feelings can hold a person hostage. How so? Well, when we resist having a feeling, we typically hold our breath. Holding your breath tells your brain that you're afraid of having that feeling. As a result, you'll start shifting down into your survival brain. (This is oftentimes the moment when people reach for food, alcohol, drugs, shopping, smoking, gossiping, rage or blame. Often our addictions are an attempt to "numb-out" and not feel uncomfortable feelings.)

It's quite normal to try to make uncomfortable feelings go away. But when you do this, you engage your defense systems. Typically people shut down, go into denial, or get angry – and often it's happening outside of their conscious awareness. Sometimes your body will alert you to your deeper feelings. A classic example would be when someone asks you how you are, and you snap back with *"I'm fine!"* You might surprise yourself (and others) with your gruff tone, at which point you'll probably realize that maybe you're not so fine after all.

We all have uncomfortable feelings that we try to avoid. The list is different for each of us. One person might want to avoid feeling ashamed, humiliated, or angry, and another might avoid feeling shy, guilty or afraid. Whatever the case, it's usually tied to the messages we received when we were young children. Some of those messages may be limiting in ways that we don't enjoy, don't want to live with anymore, and don't want to pass along to our children.

As you develop more awareness and engage new skills, you can choose which messages to keep and which to let go of.

Make friends with your uncomfortable feelings.

Getting comfortable having uncomfortable feelings will help keep you out of your survival brain. As you get more comfortable with the experience of feeling uncomfortable feelings, those feelings will no longer hold as much power over you. With practice, you'll notice that you are no longer incapacitated when those uncomfortable feelings surface.

As soon as you learn that you can have an uncomfortable feeling and be safe – at the same time – the trance will automatically be released, and those uncomfortable feelings won't have you in their grip any more.

As always, breathing is essential. When you have a feeling that is uncomfortable, breathe. Focus on the exhale. Your deep, slow exhalation triggers the discomfort to release.

Comfortable Feeling	*I can allow myself to feel it* - Yes or No
Uncomfortable Feeling	*I can allow myself to feel it* - Yes or No

Can you see how much feelings, breathing, and self-talk are all linked together? Uncomfortable feelings arise. They're a normal part of life. There is a tendency to tell yourself, consciously or unconsciously, that the feeling that is surfacing is not safe to feel – and as a result, you hold your breath and downshift into your survival brain. When this happens, you get a flood of stress chemicals that actually intensify the uncomfortable feelings, thus they get even more intense. What might have been a mildly uncomfortable moment can shift into a full-on panic, all because of impaired breathing. When this occurs, people commonly become angry, anxious, or they shut down. This is frequently the point when people will impulsively act out in physical or verbal rage.

Unpacking Anger

Lots of people confuse anger with violence. But they're not the same thing. Anger is a feeling. Violence is a behavior. Most of the time when people feel angry they hold their breath, prompting a downshift into survival brain. Then they react with some corresponding behavior – perhaps a snide remark, or they might just walk away without any explanation. Or they might become heated and get rough or violent – verbally, emotionally or physically.

Anger is also a signal. It indicates that there is an important need that's not being met. There is a common error people make when they identify that their needs are not being met. We blame others. We forget that *we* are responsible for getting our needs met, and that we have options for how to do that.

The trick is to get back into your thinking brain, so you *can* connect with your resourceful, creative-thinking abilities. From your thinking brain, you're *able* to find options. When you're in survival mode, your perspective narrows, and you *literally* cannot generate or recognize possibilities. (Your perspective could change quite dramatically as soon as you shift back into your thinking brain.)

Please note: anger is a secondary emotion – it masks the three primary emotions: fear, pain, and sadness. Often those primary emotions can be too uncomfortable to express, or even to feel. Anger comes up when we're afraid.

One way to cut through your anger is to take a couple of slow deep breaths. Notice the moment just before you feel angry. Can you identify that prior feeling? Ask yourself, "*What's the fear? What so painful? What am I sad about?*" You may find that the underlying cause is not in this moment – it may be about some unresolved past event or a projected future moment.

An

angry

person is a

frightened

person.

So what do you do with anger?

1. Identify what the underlying fear, pain, or sadness might be.

2. Identify what you can do to constructively address the underlying issue. What actions can you take to create a solution rather than just venting and remaining in the distress?

When Therapy Might Be Something To Consider

If you feel cynical and jaded – if you see life as a struggle – it could be an indication that you would benefit by addressing some underlying, unhealed issues.

Lots of people have experienced trauma or significant feelings of overwhelm as a child. For these individuals, trying to imagine that life could feel great is nearly impossible.

If you experienced trauma as a child and the issues remain unresolved, odds are that you will (unconsciously) spend much of your adult life trying to protect yourself, a survival brain function. Regardless of when that trauma occurred, even if it was fifty years ago, until it's resolved there will be a part of your survival brain that stays on alert and keeps attending to the issue, in a dedicated effort to keep you safe in case the trauma were to occur again. This constant scanning keeps you in survival mode. As a result your body experiences tension, illness, and fatigue, and your thinking becomes impaired in its ability to remain calm, clear, and focused. You may experience this as frequently feeling anxious, angry, overwhelmed, or you may even become physically sick.

The survival brain can't make the shift itself into generating solutions or happiness. That's not its job. *Solutions and happiness are generated by your thinking brain.* Therapy allows you to resolve the issue and develop a coping strategy so that your survival brain does not feel the need to stay in defense around that issue.

There are many forms of therapy that are effective at helping people resolve past traumas and issues. Some involve dialogue, others focus on working with the body to achieve release, and some utilize energetic adjustments for yourself or the whole family system to facilitate relief. There are many methods to choose from, and no single method is right for everyone. The criterion in assessing a right fit for you is to notice if you are getting the outcomes you want. If you are, great! If you're not, try another approach – and keep trying until you find one that's a good fit for you. The end result is worth the effort. *You deserve a life that feels great on a regular basis.*

Strategies To Change a Feeling

Each of the following strategies uses a different mechanism to shift uncomfortable feelings. Give each a try, and identify the ones that work best for you.

1. Uncomfortable feelings are telling you to stop and look at your own thinking and behavior. Uncomfortable feelings are your body's way of letting you know that your focus is turned in the wrong direction. Uncomfortable feelings are a signal alerting you to the fact that something important is out of balance. Discomfort can be seen as a call to restore balance. Identify what is out of balance. Pause for a moment and reflect on your thinking and your actions. What is blocking your alignment with your goals, dreams or values? After you've identified the mismatch, shift your focus to what you *do* want, and start to generate the thinking and actions that will get you there. You'll notice that when you've realigned your thoughts and behaviors with your goals, dreams, and values your emotions will be much more comfortable.

2. Go for gratitude. One of the fastest ways to shift into more comfortable emotions is to focus on what you're grateful for. It might be your health, or your home, your family, your work, your hobbies, your friends, etc. Even though all of the details of your life may not be exactly as you wish, you *do* have things that are working. Shifting your focus to what you are grateful for (and off of what you don't have yet) will shift your emotions. You have much to be grateful for. Look for it.

3. Get up and move. If you're stuck in a negative feeling, you're stuck in your body. Time to move! Go for a five-minute walk – taking long strides. Or go get a glass of water. Even one minute of movement will help. Wash your hands and splash your face with water. Go outside and get some fresh air. Do a favorite yoga pose. Lift some weights for a few minutes. See how quickly you can walk around the block. Throw the ball with your dog. Move...

4. Turn on the music. Listen to music that you love – whatever makes you want to sing, dance, laugh, or cry – music you connect with.

5. Balance your brain. Do some Cross-Crawls to "reset" your brain. Here's how:

- Stand up.

- Lower your left elbow and simultaneously raise your right knee until they touch.

- Then reverse – lower your right elbow and raise your left knee till they touch.

- Repeat 7 times on each side — 14 times total.

6. Change your focus. A basic rule of physics is whatever you focus on expands. Your brain will create more of whatever you're thinking about. If you are thinking about your stress, your brain will create more stress. If you're focused on solutions, your brain will create more solutions. Focus your attention on what you *do* want, rather than on what you *don't* want. Change your focus and you'll change your feeling.

It's useful to remember that your brain has trouble processing negatives, so you'll want to remember to phrase your self-talk as positive statements. For example, instead of saying *"I'm done with feeling frustrated all the time"* you might say *"I'm so glad I can have disappointments and still have a good productive day."*

7. Stop resisting. What you resist persists. Allow yourself to feel uncomfortable feelings. Doing so will give those feelings an opportunity to deliver their valuable feedback, and then they can move through and pass on. Remind yourself, *"Even though I feel _____ I am okay just the way I am."* You can replace *"okay"* with whatever is a match for you: *"I am safe, loved, competent, capable, valuable, etc."* This type of self-talk will remove the resistance, and it will allow your survival brain to come off-guard. Productive self-talk facilitates shifting gears.

8. Breathe. Notice your breathing when you are having an uncomfortable feeling. Odds are that you are holding your breath or engaging only shallow upper-chest breathing, which activates your survival brain and actually increases that uncomfortable feeling. When you slowly exhale from deep down in your belly, you'll release the uncomfortable feelings. *The slower you breathe, the more comfortable you'll get.*

Increase Your Awareness:

- *How would you like to feel more frequently?*

- *What self-talk can you use to create those feelings?*

- *What feelings do you want to get more comfortable having?*

Practice Feeling Your Feelings:

Know you're safe.

- Identify a feeling that you dislike having.

- Breathe deeply.

- Allow yourself to feel that feeling for five seconds.

- Then say to yourself: *"Even though I feel _____, I am okay just the way I am."*

- Now focus your awareness on something that you enjoy or appreciate right here, right now. Bring your awareness into the present moment.

Breathe into the feeling.

- When you notice an uncomfortable feeling arising, stop for a moment. Just "pause" on taking any action.

- Begin belly breathing.

- Feel the feeling... Inhale deeply, and exhale slowly... Don't resist the feeling or try to make it go away... Just feel it.

- As you continue to breathe and feel the feeling, double the length of your exhalation.

- Repeat six times. Feel it, and exhale fully...

- Now check again. Notice what's happening to that uncomfortable feeling.

Focus on the feelings you prefer.

You create more of whatever you give your attention to – positive or negative. How would you like to feel? What do you prefer? What do you want your experience to be today? *(Confident, strong, peaceful, content, happy, etc.)* Focus your attention in those directions. Remember, what you think about you bring about.

Do a mental rehearsal.

- Identify an emotion that is uncomfortable for you to feel. Pick one that is a known challenge for you – one that usually triggers you to respond with anger or anxiety when it surfaces, or perhaps one that causes you to reach for food or a cigarette.

- In your imagination, see yourself having this feeling unexpectedly, and see yourself remembering to breathe. As you maintain your breathing, give yourself permission to feel the feeling. Recognize that you can feel this feeling and be calm and feel safe, all at the same time.

- Repeat three or four times.

- Stay with it until you can breathe in and out slowly, deeply, and easily.

- When you can imagine this situation and achieve a full, deep exhalation at the same time, it indicates that you have integrated your new skill.

Parenting Tip:

Your child follows your model of how to manage uncomfortable feelings.

As a parent, when you are having a feeling that is uncomfortable for you, it's written all over your body language. It can be confusing for your child.

You can help your child learn to identify and manage their own uncomfortable emotions by modeling *how* to have uncomfortable feelings.

The next time you feel angry, recognize it and say out loud. *"Huh, I'm noticing that I'm feeling kind of angry. So this is a good time to take a deep breath. I'm going to calm myself down, and figure out what's bugging me."*

When your child is upset, you can help him practice staying in his thinking brain. If he is having a tantrum you can say, *"It's okay to feel upset."*

It's important that you to stay calm when your child has uncomfortable emotions. It might require a bit of self-talk, such as *"Even though my kid is upset and it's uncomfortable for me, I am okay just the way I am. I can deal with this."*

Teach your child that feelings are normal. Even uncomfortable feelings are normal and healthy and safe to feel.

...But Act From Your Values

Everyone has a certain way they want to be, and they feel good about themselves when they are that way. When we are being who we want to be, our actions are lined up with our values. When we're lined up consistently "in integrity" with ourselves, we develop greater confidence and self-esteem. We are operating from our thinking brain.

However, when we act from a strong feeling "in the heat of the moment" we are operating from our survival brain. Survival brain behaviors do not take into account any thought or awareness of our own values or other people's needs. In survival mode, we tend to be reactive. We can also be quite unpredictable, inconsistent, and even harmful. We recognize and identify this sort of behavior as being "out of control."

The survival brain is chemically and biologically disconnected from the thinking brain. They are mutually exclusive modes of operation. So, if you think about it, emotionally charged impulsive actions are literally "thoughtless."

When our behavior has been driven by our survival brain, we often "wake up" later and kick ourselves for behaving that way. We find that we don't really like ourselves as much as before, and often others don't like us so much either.

For example, meet Jane. Her reputation precedes her. Jane is renowned for her moods. Her coworkers never know what to expect. Will she be happy and generous, or angry and critical? Clearly, her emotions drive her behaviors.

So what happens when everyone is walking around on eggshells being really careful to not "trigger" Jane? Odds are they're being extra careful and cautious, and perhaps they're a bit afraid – all survival brain indicators. At least some of those people are likely to forget to breathe, or they will drop into sparse, shallow breathing. Maintaining a pervasive level of cautiousness impairs people's ability to breathe, and the resulting lack of oxygen activates their survival brain. Given the automatic dynamics of emotional contagion, fear can spread quickly.

Walking around on eggshells not only detracts from experiencing your environment as safe, it also impedes optimal learning. This can pose a real problem, because most environments (whether it's a classroom, a workplace, or a home) require that we engage in some level of ongoing learning, relating, and teamwork on a regular basis.

Values Are Enduring

Usually our values are set early in life. They are the principles, standards, and qualities that we hold as desirable and worthwhile. Values are generally consistent and predictable.

Though values are different for every person and they vary from one culture to another, there are some values that are held by many people. Honesty, freedom, reverence for life, respect, responsibility, fairness and compassion are all widely commonly held values.

When we act from our values, we choose behaviors that are consistent with those values, *regardless of our feeling or mood in the moment.*

For example…

• *When Amanda realizes that a few of her team members have not followed through and they're going to miss the deadline, she begins to get really angry. As she starts to assign blame, she feels her jaw tightening and her shoulders tensing up. Recognizing her physical cues, she stops, takes a deep breath and decides to redirect her thinking. She goes over to meet with her team leaders and opens the dialogue to figure out what the options are. In so doing, she is demonstrating her values: collaboration, respect, and commitment to getting the job done.*

- *Bill is often frustrated when he has the kids for the weekend. It feels like chaos in the house – kids, toys, the dog... it adds up to a lot of noise! Bill has been working on connecting feelings and values. When he gets overwhelmed and just wants to explode, he knows he needs to remove himself for a moment. He takes five minutes alone, and then comes back to engage the family scene. He remembers how important it is to him to be a respectful, loving and fun dad. (And to be kind to the dog.) The kids win – he'll play with them for a while, then they can all go for a swim and take the dog for a walk. He's salvage the weekend... he can finish up that report on Monday.*

- *When Roberta walks in after a hard day at work and finds that there are dirty dishes piled high (again), she calmly reminds herself to have a conversation with the kids about after-school expectations. Roberta really values quality family communications and respectful family relations. She is committed to teaching her children about consequences, being accountable, and keeping agreements. She can see that this cam be turned into a learning moment.*

We all exist amidst a confluence of many values in every moment. But we don't generally walk around thinking about our values.

How can you hone in on what your values are? Look at your behaviors. Your behaviors show you what you value. They provide constant clues about what your values really are.

Look at your behaviors and your use of time and money.
It will tell you a lot about what your most important values are.

We all grew up with family values. Whether or not they were overtly defined, they did (and still do) exist. All families have values. As children, we are imprinted with our family's values, which are in turn related to our parent's experience of their childhood, and so on.

As we move into and navigate through adulthood we can consciously select our own core values. Choosing your own values is part of the maturation process. Often people will keep some of the values they grew up with, perhaps drop some, and perhaps add new values. Often we're not aware that we've had any shift in our values until we have some experience that tips us off to a new awareness.

Developing more consciousness about what we value is quite useful. It brings forward our sense of self, we gain greater clarity about what motivates our lives, and it allows us to generate and engage in more satisfying activities and relationships.

What are your values?

Excellence	Accountability
Independence	Trust
Creativity	Competition
Kindness	Optimism
Honesty	Education
Loyalty	Community
Reliability	Spirituality
Comfort	Fairness
Health	Cleanliness
Safety	Freedom
Precision	Fun
Teamwork	*(There are plenty more… add your own…)*

Increase Your Awareness:

- *Begin to notice who and what you admire. What values do those people consistently demonstrate, regardless of what's going on around them or within them? What qualities or values do they embody that you admire?*

- *What values would you like to be known for?*

- *Which do you consistently act on now?*

- *Which values do you abandon when you get stressed or angry?*

- *Which values would you like to act from, regardless of your emotional state?*

- *Which values are most important to you?*

Remember…

You can have

strong and uncomfortable feelings

and still choose behaviors

that are in alignment

with your values.

It's worth repeating...

Feel your feelings,

but

act from your values.

Impulse Control

The ability to have impulse control when a strong feeling occurs is a hallmark of maturity and professionalism.

Impulse control boils down to distinguishing between feelings and values in the heat of the moment, and then choosing behaviors that demonstrate your values.

Impulse control is the critical skill that separates mature from immature individuals, and professional from unprofessional behaviors.

Here are some examples of impulsive actions:

- *rolling your eyes when you've heard or seen something you don't like*
- *walking out on the conversation or hanging up on a phone call*
- *getting loud or belligerent*
- *using accusatory language (guilt, shame, blame)*
- *behaving like a bully*
- *making polite threats or issuing ultimatums*
- *gossiping*
- *addictive or out-of-control behavior patterns – eating, drinking, shopping, gambling, smoking*

Increase Your Awareness:

Do you know what your particular impulsive tendencies are? What triggers your impulsive behaviors? What do you need to avoid saying or doing when you get worked-up? *(If you're not sure, ask the people around you. They'll know!)*

Impulse control is simply navigating the shift from your survival brain to your thinking brain.

Impulse control requires developing the skill of self-awareness. When we have self-awareness, we recognize our internal dialogue (what we say to ourselves), and we're able to connect our self-talk with our emotions and reactions.

Self-awareness comes from your thinking brain.

The next time you find yourself in a situation that is challenging or otherwise triggering, use it as an opportunity to practice impulse control.

Step-By-Step Impulse Control

1. Be still. Stop all actions.

2. Zip your lips. Be silent.

3. Lengthen and deepen your breathing. Two quick ways to get there are:
   - Lie down on the floor or another hard surface and belly breathe for a full three minutes. *Or...*
   - Get active for a full three minutes. Do jumping jacks or take a brisk walk, swinging your arms fully. Aim for deep breathing and big arm movements.

4. Get in control of your thinking. Use proactive, productive self-talk. *(See p 42-43.)*

5. Identify the values you would like your actions to communicate in this situation.

6. Exhale slowly... then proceed.

Practice Acting From Your Values:

1. Think about your values. Notice how your behavior and your words communicate or don't communicate your values. What would it take to bring your values into action more regularly?

2. Do a mental rehearsal.

- Identify a situation in which you lose self control and act in ways you do not admire.

- Identify how you would like to think and act instead.

- In your imagination, see yourself in the same situation – but this time, acting from your values.

- Repeat three or four times.

- Stay with it until you can breathe in and out slowly, deeply, and easily.

- When you can imagine this situation and achieve a full, deep exhalation at the same time, it indicates that you have integrated your new skill.

3. Practice in the real world. Put yourself in a situation where you are inclined to get upset or irritated. Practice staying calm, respectful, and collaborative.

Putting It
All Together

Putting It All Together
[make life easier]

You've just taken in a lot of information. It may help your learning retention and integration to remember that it all boils down to one concept and four skills.

- Concept: **Understand how your brain works.** *Develop the ability to shift gears and access your thinking brain.*

- Skill 1: **Breathe.** *Into and out of your belly... slow and deep, with full exhalations.*

- Skill 2: **Listen to what you are saying, to yourself and others.** *Your thinking and your language choices will direct your course. Steer yourself in the direction you want to go.*

- Skill 3: **Repair your injured relationships.** *Apologize, using the "What I would do different next time..." model.*

- Skill 4: **Feel your feelings, but act from your values.** *Make friends with the experience of having feelings, even uncomfortable feelings. Practice impulse control. Choose behaviors that are in alignment with your values.*

You can start slow. Try choosing one skill each day, and see where you can apply it.

Begin simply. Work with your breathing. Before you get out of bed in the morning, take five deep, slow belly breaths. Notice your breathing as you shower, when you make breakfast, and when you are thinking about what you need to get done today. Just notice and play with it.

Allow your body to inform you when you are or are not breathing properly. If you notice a headache developing, tension in your stomach, or a kink in your neck, these are signals from your body that your muscles are starving for oxygen. The cure is simple: *breathe...*

If you find yourself getting irritable, judgmental, whiney or complaining, check your breathing. These attitudes are giving you the feedback that you are producing too many stress hormones. Are you belly breathing?

Notice and celebrate your accomplishments. Congratulate yourself when you remember to breathe and calm down instead of snapping at your child, coworker, or spouse.

Consider finding a friend or co-worker who wants to buddy up with you on cultivating these skills. Support each other. Instead of gossiping during breaks, take a quick walk and talk about the positives in your lives. Encourage each other to hydrate throughout the day, especially around 3:00 PM, when our bodies needs it most.

When the Process Becomes Uncomfortable

If you find yourself caught up in feelings that leave you off balance (anxious, angry, sad or afraid), consider using a few of these tools:

Feel your feelings. Remind yourself that it is normal to have whatever feelings are occurring. Identify and acknowledge what you are feeling. Remind yourself that you really can have uncomfortable feelings *and be safe* – at the same time.

Breathe. When you get stuck in an uncomfortable emotion, chances are also you're stuck in a shallow breathing pattern. Remember, shallow exhalations increase the chemicals that produce stress feelings. Exhale from deep in your belly.

Get up and move. Take a five-minute walk. Stretch. Go get a glass of water. Moving your body frequently during the day will help you maintain a better emotional balance.

Notice what you are saying to yourself. Release any inner dialogue that perpetuates fear, sadness, or anger. Choose self-talk that acknowledges your feelings and still allows you to maintain a sense of inner calm.

Choose your conversations with others. We have a tendency to bond through shared pain. Notice your conversations… do they help you and others heal, or do they expand the pain?

Be grateful. Make a list of what you are grateful for in your life. Put this list where you can see it easily this week.

Music helps. Listen to music that inspires you. Choose those songs that move you to laughter, smiles, tears, or any emotion that is *real* for you.

Allow your tears. If you feel sad and you need to cry, find a private spot and allow yourself those tears. Crying is a normal, healthy way to relieve stress and toxins. Crying re-balances your thinking. When needed, a three-minute cry can fix your whole day.

Connect. If it's a fit for you, perform a small ritual. Set aside some time to reflect. Light a candle. Send your form of love or prayer to surround yourself and others who might need it. Reach out to support someone else who may be hurting. Take a few moments to envision a better future.

Remember Your Q-TIP Q - Quit T - Taking I - It P - Personally *What other people say and do is about their wants and needs.* **Don't make it personal.** *It's NOT about you.*

How to Help Others:

- When someone else is in survival mode, try to remember that it's not about you. What people say and do is about *their* needs and *their* wants. Remain in your thinking brain when others are in their survival brain.

- Notice your breathing. Get your breath, so they can get theirs.

- Fully engage your listening. Two minutes of being heard can bring people back to their thinking brain.

- Acknowledge and validate their feelings and their reality.

- Ask what they need right now. Help them identify their needs.

- Don't judge. Remember, everyone has problems they feel overwhelmed by at times.

- Go for a walk together.

- Add humor. Inspire laughter.

- Find something you admire about them in that moment. Tell them.

- Be aware of your modeling. Stay calm, relaxed and engaged – even if they're not.

How to Help Yourself:

- Breathe.

- Listen – to yourself and others.

- Have fun with your learning. While these ideas are certainly potent, they don't need to be heavy. Play with it. Make it fun. Learn to laugh at yourself and with others.

- Drink plenty of water. Within five minutes of drinking four ounces of water, your cortisol levels will drop. [Cortisol is one of the stress chemicals.]

- Deepen your breathing, frequently. Within just one minute of shifting into long, slow, deep exhalations you'll begin to notice a change in your mood and attitude, and your stress chemicals will start to drop. For even greater benefit, belly breathe for two to five minutes.

- While 97% of our lives work well, we tend to focus on and bond with others over the 3% that doesn't. Practice choosing conversations that focus on the 97%.

- Go for gratitude. We've all got plenty to be grateful for. What's on your list today?

Forgive yourself.

Forgive each other.

Try again.

Hang in there. You can do it.

Index

Robin Rose is a trainer, consultant, and keynote speaker who specializes in *helping people bring their best selves forward*. Her work is based on an in-depth understanding of brain based research, with a particular focus on high-function brain states.

Robin connects cutting-edge scientific information with an uncommon understanding of individual and group process. She has taught thousands of people *how* to engage their challenging moments with greater power, ability, and ease. In classrooms and board rooms, with groups large and small, Robin trains people *how* to override the fight-or-flight response, *how* to shift from reactive impulses into more effective responses, and *how* to stay respectful, productive, and professional.

Robin consults with a wide array of corporations, small businesses, educational institutions and nonprofit organizations, as well as social service, healthcare and government agencies. She works with teams and key leaders to enhance skills, integrate new behaviors, and improve performance. Robin holds a master's degree in counseling psychology from Lewis & Clark College, and has been teaching, training, and consulting since 1985.

To order additional copies of this book,
please visit the website:

www.robinrose.com

On the home page you can sign up for
Robin's FREE e-newsletter, Stay*Well*.

You'll also find plenty of information about
Robin's consulting, training and keynote speaking,
as well as additional products and helpful
articles you can download free of charge.

44059667R00078

Made in the USA
San Bernardino, CA
06 January 2017